Rabbit

Written by
Matthew Rayner BVetMed MRCVS

Photographed by
Jane Burton

Gareth Stevens Publishing
A WORLD ALMANAC EDUCATION GROUP COMPANY

Please visit our web site at: www.garethstevens.com
For a free color catalog describing Gareth Stevens
Publishing's list of high-quality books and multi-
media programs, call 1-800-542-2595 (USA)
or 1-800-387-3178 (Canada). Gareth Stevens
Publishing's fax: (414) 332-3567.

Library of Congress Cataloging-in-Publication Data

Rayner, Matthew.
    Rabbit / written by Matthew Rayner;
photographed by Jane Burton. — North
American ed.
        p. cm. — (I am your pet)
    Includes bibliographical references and index.
    Summary: Presents simple information about
rabbits and choosing one as a pet.
    ISBN 0-8368-4105-0 (lib. bdg.)
    1. Rabbits—Juvenile literature. [1. Rabbits.
2. Pets.] I. Burton, Jane, ill. II. Title.
SF453.2.R38   2004
636.932'2—dc22   2003066156

This North American edition first published in 2004 by
Gareth Stevens Publishing
A World Almanac Education Group Company
330 West Olive Street, Suite 100
Milwaukee, WI 53212 USA

Original edition copyright © 2004 Bookwork Ltd.,
Unit 17, Piccadilly Mill, Lower Street, Stroud,
Gloucestershire, GL5 2HT, United Kingdom.

Editorial Director:
  Louise Pritchard
Editor: Annabel Blackledge
Design Director: Jill Plank
Art Editor: Kate Mullins
Gareth Stevens Editor:
  Jenette Donovan Guntly
Gareth Stevens Designer:
  Kami M. Koenig

Printed in the
United States of America

1 2 3 4 5 6 7 8 9 08 07 06 05 04

Picture credits
t=top, b=bottom, m=middle, l=left, r=right
All photographs by Jane Burton except for the
following: Warren Photographic: 7tr, 7tm, 7mr, 8br,
9t, 10tr, 17br, 19tr, 27tm, 27b, 28ml, 28br, 29t, 29br

Ooooh,
I've got to look
my best!

Contents

Words that appear in the glossary are printed in **boldface** type the first time they are used in the text.

My family

I come from a family of animals called **lagomorphs**. My closest relatives are wild rabbits and hares. I am just one of the many beautiful types of pet rabbits.

Are you ready to learn all about me?

Cottontail
I have a short, fluffy tail. It is white underneath. Wild rabbits flash their tails to warn their friends of danger.

Furry coat
All rabbits have thick fur. My fur is short, but some pet rabbits have long fur.

Vital statistics

I am a medium-size rabbit. I was fully grown when I was eight months old. Most pet rabbits live for between five and eight years, but some live for more than ten years. I hope I have a long and happy life with you!

Here I am

Back legs
I have very strong back legs. They help me to jump and run fast.

I am a good listener.

Ear we go
I have big, long ears. They are very good at picking up sounds. I can hear things that you cannot hear.

Built for speed
I can run fast and jump high. I need plenty of space to play in. If I am cooped up for a long time, I will feel sad and my long, strong legs will get stiff and weak.

Buck teeth
I have long front teeth to grasp food and strong back teeth to grind it up. My teeth will keep growing all my life.

Twitchy nose
I have a good sense of smell. I use it to find out about other rabbits. All rabbits rub their chins on things to leave their scent. You cannot smell it, but we can.

Fluffy feet
I have five toes on my front paws and four on my back paws. I have claws on all my toes to help me dig and grip the ground when I run.

All shapes and sizes

Pet rabbits come in lots of shapes, sizes, and colors. Each type of rabbit is called a **breed**. Small rabbits can weigh as little as 2 pounds (1 kilogram). Large ones can weigh 22 pounds (10 kg).

Bunny breeds

Little characters
Different breeds of rabbits have different characters. The larger breeds are usually quieter than the smaller breeds.

Hello, my floppy-eared friend!

Dwarf Lop
My bunny friend is a Dwarf Lop. Dwarf Lops have long, floppy ears and are the most popular breed of pet rabbit.

Angora
This is an Angora rabbit. She has a very long, fluffy coat. Even her ears are fluffy!

English Spot
My English Spot friend is named after his coat. It is white with spots. He is a medium-size rabbit like me.

All kinds of ears
All rabbits have wonderful ears, but many of us have extra special ears. Some are floppy. Some stand up straight. Some are furry, and some are pointed. Some are tiny, and some are huge.

Netherland Dwarf
The Netherland Dwarf is one of the smallest rabbits and has tiny, pointed ears.

All mixed up
I am not a **pedigreed** bunny. My parents were different breeds. I still am just as beautiful as my pedigreed friends!

Back to nature

Wild ways

Pet rabbits like me behave in
a similar way to our wild cousins.
We are lively and like to explore.
We prefer to eat first thing in the
morning and in the early evening,
which are the safest times in the wild.

LOOK OUT!

- **Do not** chase me
  when you want to
  pick me up. I may
  think you are hunting
  me. The more you
  chase me, the faster
  I will run.

Always alert

We never stop
listening for sounds
of danger.

Ready to run

Rabbits can
spring into
action in a
split second.
We can run
very fast to
escape from
danger, too.

Dig deep

We do not need to
dig **burrows** to
live in, but we will
still have fun digging
if you let us play
outside in the yard.

Thumper
If I am scared, I may thump a back foot on the ground. Wild rabbits do this to warn their friends of danger nearby. It could be a fox hunting for his dinner!

Wild relations

Rabbits like to be with other rabbits. In the wild, they live together in burrows underground. During the day, they come out to eat and play. They like to **groom** each other, too.

Somewhere to live

Before you bring me home, you need to buy me a **hutch**. It must be large enough for me to hop around in. If you keep me outside, make sure my hutch protects me from the wind and rain. I will also need a large outdoor **run**.

Getting ready

House rabbit

The best place for me to live is inside your house. I will need a special indoor hutch to live in, but you can let me out to play when you are there to watch me.

Litter bunny

You can train me to use a litter box. Buy one that is large enough for me to sit in. You will also need special rabbit litter. Put the box where I usually go to the bathroom.

Tenderfoot

Hutches with wire floors can hurt my feet. Line my hutch with thick cardboard or wood and straw.

It's such thirsty work being a superstar!

Bunny bottle
You can get a special bottle for my water. It will clip to my hutch and will not spill as a bowl might.

Grooming kit
Buy a special rabbit brush for grooming me. Longhaired rabbits need to be groomed every day.

Food for thought
I will need a bowl that will not break if I throw it around. I will also need food, hay, and some fresh vegetables to nibble each day.

Which rabbit?

Which rabbit?

LOOK OUT!

- **Never choose** a rabbit that has a wet nose or eyes or is very thin. He may be sick.
- **If you** choose a female rabbit, ask if she is going to have babies before you buy her. You do not want to have more rabbits than you expected!

Places to go

Buy your rabbit from an animal shelter or a breeder. You can find rabbits through the newspaper or from notices found in pet shops, too. Your **veterinarian**, or vet, may also have some notices.

Full of life
I am alert and lively. Choose a rabbit like me, not one that is very sleepy or quiet.

Fine fur
I keep my fur clean, so it is always soft and shiny. Your rabbit should have fur like mine.

Of course I've washed behind my ears!

I think we'd be perfect together!

Boys and girls

Sometimes, boy and girl rabbits act differently. Each rabbit's character is different, too. You should spend time getting to know a rabbit before you choose him or her.

Friendly
Choose a friendly rabbit like me. I am playful and I love being petted.

All grown up
I am grown up and **house trained**. I am already tame, too. I am less work than a baby bunny.

Checkup
Take me to the vet for a checkup as soon as you get me. The vet will tell you whether I need medicine or not and will give you advice about caring for me.

Feed me!

Hooray for hay

The most important part of my
diet is good-quality hay. Make sure
I always have plenty of fresh hay and
I will nibble on it happily all day.

Twice as nice!
Do not be worried if I eat
my droppings. I do this to
get as much nutrition out
of my food as possible.

> **LOOK OUT!**
> • **Never feed** me chocolate, sweet food, or
>   mown grass. They will upset my tummy.
> • **Do not** let me get too fat. I will not be
>   able to clean myself properly and
>   might get an infection.

Oh goody,
my favorite treat
. . . an apple.

Fresh and fruity

I like to nibble the lawn, but
be sure no chemicals have
been put on it. Growing
grass is good for
my teeth and
digestion. If
you have
no lawn, I
should eat
fresh fruit or
vegetables.

Less is more
Feed me only small amounts of
fruit. Half an apple a day is plenty.
Any more could upset my tummy.

Fruit and
vegetables

Mixed food

Pellets

Be prepared
Besides hay, you
can feed me small
amounts of pellets
or mixed rabbit
food from a pet
shop. Hay should
still be the
main part
of my
diet.

Drink up
I need to have fresh water
to drink all the time. It helps
me to digest my food properly.
Please change my drinking
water every day.

Delicate tummy
If you want to change my diet,
do it gradually. A sudden
change will make me sick.

Naturally clean

I am naturally a clean animal. I will go to the bathroom mainly in one area of my hutch. If you train me to use a litter box, it will be easy to keep my hutch clean.

Aspen wood shavings

Hay

All the right stuff
When you clean out my hutch, you will need to give me a fresh layer of dust-free **bedding**, fresh food, and a pile of hay to sleep in.

A tidy home

Why and when

You must clean out my hutch at least once a week. Dirty bedding can give me sore feet and breathing problems. It also attracts flies in the summer. The flies will lay eggs on me, which will make me very sick.

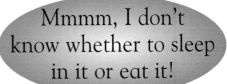

Mmmm, I don't know whether to sleep in it or eat it!

LOOK OUT!

• **Do not** use cedar or pine wood shavings or scented or treated wood shavings. They may hurt my liver, irritate my eyes and lungs, or make my feet sore. Use aspen wood shavings or paper pellets instead.

The know-how

Put me in a safe place while you clean out my hutch. Wipe it down with weak disinfectant. Never use bleach or other strong chemical cleaners. They will burn my skin and paws. After you finish, let my hutch dry out.

Scoop it up
Use a scoop to take droppings and any wet bedding out of my hutch every day.

Freshen up
If you give me hay to sleep in, I will probably eat most of it. Give me a large handful of fresh hay each day.

I am all ears!

Reading the signs

Rabbits talk to each other using their bodies. I will talk to you this way, too. As you get to know me, you will learn my **body language**. Then you will know when I am happy, angry, or scared, just from the way I behave.

Nasty noises

If I am angry or scared, I may growl or hiss. I might even charge at you and try to bite you. If I am badly injured, you might hear me scream.

Who's there?

If I stand up tall with my ears pricked, it means that I am feeling alert and curious.

LOOK OUT!

- If I am very quiet and grind my teeth, I may be sick or in pain. Take me to the vet.
- If I become naughty or mean, I may be bored. Play with me more and give me things to do in my hutch.

Bunny bliss

When I am happy, I often purr like a cat. You may hear me purr when you stroke and groom me. If I am pleased to see you or want to play, I will chase you or jump around.

Chilling out
When a rabbit is tired or just very relaxed, she will flop down on the floor and spread herself out.

Rabbit habits

Clean noses are best for twitching.

Wash time
I groom myself and my bunny friends only when I feel relaxed and safe. If you are lucky, I might try to groom you, too!

Making friends

I may be shy when you first get me. You must give me time to get to know you. When I feel I can trust you, I will let you handle me. Do not try to pick me up until I am ready. Wait for me to come to you.

A friend for life

Oooh, don't stop. That feels wonderful!

The gentle touch
Stroke me gently on my head. This lets me know that you only want to be my friend and will not hurt me.

LOOK OUT!
- **Never try** to grab me. You will startle me.
- **Never pick** me up by my ears. This will hurt me.
- **Never hit** me if I have been naughty. I will not know what I have done wrong, and you will just frighten me.

Pick me up

You must pick me up properly so that you do not hurt my back. Put one hand under my bottom. Hold on to my chest with your other hand so that you do not drop me.

Carry me

Being carried may scare me or hurt me. If you must hold me, wrap me in a towel. It will help me feel safe. Hold me gently, close to your body. If I struggle, put me down.

Rabbit treats and chews

Training treats

When you are training me or making friends, give me a tasty treat to help me understand. You can use pieces of fresh vegetable or fruit or treats from a pet shop.

Busy bunny

I am very curious and get bored easily if I do not have anything to eat or investigate. Give me some toys to play with and things to nibble. Let me explore new places, too.

Home and

Okay, Mr. Snail, let's have a race!

Come inside

As well as playing outside, I will enjoy being inside your home. I will sniff everything, run around, and might even lie down next to you while you are watching television.

Part of the family

I will want to be where you are. Let me follow you around while you clean your room or do your chores. I will soon feel like part of the family.

LOOK OUT!
- **Never let** me run around indoors all alone. I might ruin the furniture and carpets or hurt myself.
- **Never leave** me on my own outdoors. I might dig or chew my way out of my run or under the fence.

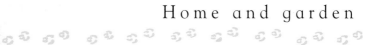

garden

The great outdoors

My wild cousins spend most of their time outside in the fresh air. I need to spend time outside, too. There is nothing I like better than nibbling a few dandelions, running around the lawn, then flopping down for a nap.

Tunnels and pots

Put tunnels and pots in my run. I will dash through them and climb on them.

No one has to tell me to eat my greens.

Playing it safe

When I am outside, keep me in a fenced yard or run and never leave me alone. This will keep me safe from foxes, cats, and dogs.

Fun with food

I am happy to spend hours each day munching on plants and grasses. You can even hide bits of food around my hutch. I love to hunt and scrabble for tasty tidbits.

Daily checkups

I will probably stay very healthy if you care for me properly, but there are some common illnesses and problems I can have. I may become very sick if you let them get worse, so give me a checkup every day. Take me to the vet at least once a year.

Health matters

Careful, that tickles!

Coat and skin
When you groom me, check that I do not have bald patches or flaky skin. If I am scratching a lot, I may have fleas or **mites**.

Getting to know me
It is very important that you get to know me well and learn all of my usual habits. Then, you will notice if I am feeling sick, because I will behave differently.

Ear checks
Look in my ears for sore spots. Check that there is not a lot of wax. Never put anything inside my ears.

Mmmm, much tastier than toothpaste!

Bright eyes
Check that my eyes are clean and bright. Sometimes my tears do not drain away properly, and this can cause problems with my eyes.

Teeth check
Give me fruit-tree twigs to chew to help keep my teeth healthy. If I am dribbling or cannot eat properly, my teeth may be hurting me.

LOOK OUT!
- **Look out** for fly eggs and **maggots** on me. They can kill me. If you see any, take me to the vet quickly.
- **Go straight** to the vet if I sneeze a lot or have a runny nose. I could have **snuffles**.

Bottom check
Check my bottom twice a day. Clean it if it is dirty. Take me to the vet to find out why it is getting dirty.

I need a friend

I need company most of the time
or I will get lonely and bored.
I like making friends with dogs,
guinea pigs, and other rabbits,
but never introduce me to a
cat. It might try to eat me!

Two's

Furry friends
I like to play
with guinea pigs,
but you should
watch us. I may
bully them.
We should
never eat
the same
food or
or sleep
in the
same
cage.

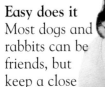

Easy does it
Most dogs and rabbits can be friends, but keep a close eye on us.

Fast learner
A puppy will learn quickly how to behave around me. She might even let me be the boss!

Company

Double bunnies
Living with another rabbit will suit me best of all.

Will you share your daisy with me?

You and me
If I live by myself, I will need you to be my best friend. You should come and say hello to me as often as you can and play with me every day.

Best friends

Two rabbits living together usually become friends. They will hop around after each other and will groom each other, too. Ask your vet for advice if your rabbits fight. Also, your vet can offer advice on keeping boy and girl rabbits together.

Mommy bunny

A female rabbit can start having babies at only four months old. A male rabbit can start breeding at five months old. Female rabbits make nests for the baby rabbits, which are called kittens.

Baby bunnies

No touching!
Never handle very young kittens or disturb their nest. The mother may get scared and reject them. Give her plenty to eat and lots of peace and quiet.

New baby

Kittens are born blind, deaf, and hairless. They drink milk from their mother. At one week, kittens have some fur, but they still cannot see or hear.

Starting out

Three-week-old kittens can see and hear. They begin to eat food but still need their mother's milk until they are six weeks old.

LOOK OUT!

- **Rabbits can** have lots of babies very quickly. It is best if your vet gives him or her an operation so he or she cannot breed babies.

I can't wait for them to leave home!

Happy families
When the kittens start to leave the nest to explore, you can begin to handle them. Young rabbits are very playful and like to investigate. They can get into trouble, so keep an eye on them.

Ready for adventure
Rabbits can be separated from their mother when they are six weeks old. They are ready to go to a new home at nine weeks old. At this stage, they look like small versions of their parents, but they still have a lot of growing to do.

Glossary

bedding
The material a rabbit sleeps on is her bedding. Aspen wood shavings topped with straw or hay make the best bedding.

body language
A rabbit is using body language when he shows what he is feeling and thinking through movement.

breed
A breed is a type of rabbit. Dwarf Lops and Angoras are just two of the many breeds of pet rabbits.

burrows
Wild rabbits live in holes in the ground called burrows.

groom
To groom is to brush an animal's fur to gently remove dust or dirt.

house trained
A house trained rabbit goes to the bathroom only in those areas she has been trained to go in.

hutch
A hutch is a special cage that is built for comfort and security.

lagomorphs
All lagomorphs, including rabbits, eat plants and have two rows of front teeth.

maggots
Maggots look like tiny worms in your rabbit's fur. If you see any, take him to the vet right away.

mites
Mites are tiny bugs that can live in a rabbit's fur or ears. If you see any, take her to the vet.

pedigreed
A pedigreed rabbit has a family that includes only rabbits of the same breed, such as all Angoras.

run
A run is an outdoor pen for your rabbit to exercise in.

snuffles
Snuffles is a serious disease. Take your rabbit to the vet if his nose is wet or if he has trouble breathing.

veterinarian (vet)
A veterinarian, or vet, is a doctor for animals, including rabbits.

Find out more . . .

Web Sites

houserabbit.org/Youth/ rabbits.htm
This site by the Youth House Rabbit Club has lots of bunny care advice and information.

www.animaland.org
This web site for the American Society for the Prevention of Cruelty to Animals (ASPCA) has games, cartoons, a pet care guide, and much more!

www.muridae.com/rabbits/ rabbittalk.html
This web site helps you learn to understand what your bunny's body language means. They sure do love to talk!

That's a lot of information!

Books

101 Facts About Rabbits. 101 Facts About Pets series. Julia Barnes (Gareth Stevens)

Caring for Your Rabbit. Caring for Your Pet series. Jill Foran (Weigl Educational Assoc.)

Index